LOST IN THE WOODS

also in the CHILD SURVIVAL series:
Adrift! — Boating safety for children
by Colleen Politano and Joan Neudecker

LOST IN THE WOODS

by
Colleen Politano

Illustrated by Doug Penhale

ICS BOOKS, Inc.
Merrillville, Indiana

JUV
GV
200.5
.P65
1993
c.3

LOST IN THE WOODS
Copyright © 1993 by Colleen Politano
Edited by Michael Coney, Porthole Press, Ltd., Sidney, B.C.
Cover art by Silk Questo Design, Sidney, B.C.
Cover design by Nancy Freeborn, Freeborn Design, Chester, CT
Text set by Manning Press, Sidney, B.C.

10 9 8 7 6 5 4 3 2 1

1st Printing 8-93, 2nd Printing 3-94,
3rd Printing 3-95

Printed in the U.S.A.

All ICS titles are printed on 50% recycled paper from
pre-consumer waste. All sheets are processed without
using acid.

Published by:
ICS BOOKS, Inc
1370 E. 86th Place
Merrillville, IN 46410
800-541-7323

Published in Canada by:
Porthole Press, Ltd.
2082 Neptune Rd.
Sidney
British Columbia V8L 5J5
Canada

Library of Congress Cataloging-in-Publication Data

Politano, Colleen, 1946-
    Lost in the woods : child survival / by Colleen Politano.
        p. cm.
    Includes index.
    ISBN 0-934802-83-1
    1. Wilderness survival--Juvenile literature. 2. Survival skills-
-Juvenile literature. I. Title.
GV200.5.P65   1993
613.6'9'083--dc20   93-25700
                                                             CIP

Contents

Acknowledgements

I could not have written *Lost in the Woods* without the help and support of others, in particular my husband Leon. Thank you, Leon. I would also like to thank Barry Casson for his patience and skill during the making of the film; and Mike Coney for his assistance with the manuscript and format.

Introduction

In October of 1978 Jamie Baxter and David Crocker went out to play after returning home from kindergarten one day, and didn't come back. After an extensive two-and-a-half day search, both the children were found.

Jamie Baxter died in the hours following the rescue.

As a teacher, I decided I should do something to help my students to be prepared in case any one of them ever got lost. My search for materials turned up nothing suitable for young children, so I decided to make my own. I began with a story that would capture the children's attention and act as a model of what a well-informed, resourceful child should do when faced with a frightening situation. To accompany the story I set up several activities illustrating the safety procedures outlined in the story, designed to allow the child to personally assess their value. As the project developed a third component emerged — information designed to assist parents and teachers in preparing children to help themselves if they became lost.

The story, the activities and the information for parents and teachers are the subject of this book. It is my hope that caring adults will enjoy the activities with children at home and at school, and that by being prepared for emergencies our children can enjoy our beautiful wild places in safety.

To my fellow teachers, who taught me
the value of creating your own teaching materials when
ready-made materials are not available.

Lost in the Woods

When Calvin and his Mom and Dad arrived at the campsite, Calvin couldn't wait to start exploring. First his Mom made him put on his red jacket with the hood tucked into the collar. Next she made him wait while she tucked a packet of raisins into his pocket. At last she let him go.

But even then she called after him. "Now don't go far!"

Mothers, said Calvin to himself as he ran off. *Always fussing. Zip up your jacket . . . Don't go too far . . . .*

He hurried through the bush, eager to see as much as he could before he had to go back. Soon he came to a tunnel under a road. It was dark, but he could see daylight at the far end.

Explore me, the tunnel seemed to say with its big mouth. *Explooooore me!*

It was spooky but safe, and soon Calvin was in the sunshine on the other side. In front of him a trail rose up the hill through the forest.

This is the way, the trail seemed to whisper. *Thisssss way!*

It was so exciting, the way the woods were talking to Calvin. These were words no grown-up would ever hear. The best was to come, however. Calvin climbed a big old log which lay across his path, and found himself beside a pool.

In the pool stood a little deer, drinking.

Calvin held his breath. The deer looked up and saw him, but it didn't run away. It watched him for a moment with big brown eyes. It was much younger than Calvin, but it wasn't afraid of him. When it had finished drinking it looked at him again, as if to say, *follow me*.

Then it walked into the forest.

Calvin followed. He wasn't tired and he didn't have to be back at the campsite yet. He'd never been so close to a real wild animal before. He was sure dad and mom would be pleased when he told them about the little deer. He wondered if he could make friends with it. It seemed very tame. Perhaps he could take it back to show mom and dad. It walked ahead of him, not very far away, following a narrow trail through the trees. Sometimes it stopped and looked back, and Calvin thought it was saying:

*Follow me, and I will show you wonderful things
in the forest, and I will be your friend.*

So he followed the little deer, sometimes walking, sometimes running to keep up. Then in the end the deer suddenly bounded away, deep into the woods and out of sight. Calvin thought he heard it cry:

Goodbye . . .

He found himself in a clearing surrounded by tall trees. The forest was quiet. Nothing was speaking to him any more. He sat on a log to catch his breath. He was alone. He remembered Mom and Dad at the campsite. Suddenly the forest didn't seem so friendly.

He stood up and looked around.

Deer can sure get around easily in the forest, he thought. *A lot easier than a person. Well . . . . Better get back to Mom and Dad.*

Calvin started walking. After a while the forest seemed to be thicker than it was before, and the bushes kept pulling at him like hands. Soon he began to wonder if he was going the right way. He wished the little deer would come back, to show him the way out of here. But the little deer had gone home to its Mom. Calvin began to wonder just where **his** Mom was.

At last he could see a place where the trees were not so thick, and he hurried towards it. Perhaps this was the campsite. He pushed through the bush and stepped into the open.

It was the same clearing he'd left behind him! He'd walked round in a circle!

Now Calvin was really frightened. There, right in front of him, was the same log he'd sat on before. Where were Mom and Dad? He sat down on the log.

He tried not to cry. He tried not to panic.
He tried to think, instead.

What to do now? Calvin had learned in school that there were a lot of things he could do for himself.

He remembered a talk in school, about two boys lost in the woods. He remembered what the teacher had said.

If you're lost you should stay in one place, so that people who are looking for you can find you.

Calvin began to eat his raisins. Dad and Mom might be looking for him already. Anyway, it was best to stay right here. But supposing they didn't find him for some time? He looked around. The trees looked tall and fierce, and there were strange noises out there. Supposing he had to stay here all night? He fought back a moment of panic. Now — what else had they said at school? And what about those things his parents had told him? And those neat experiments he'd seen?

It's very important to keep warm.

Calvin stood and zipped up his jacket. What next?

It's important to keep your head warm, too. What was that experiment? *Lids on, lids off*, the teacher had called it. The experiment with the pots. The teacher used it to show the children why hats were so important.

Calvin worked the hood out from under his
collar, pulled it over his head and tied it under
his chin.

Then he sat down again, keeping his hands warm and snug in his pockets. It was getting darker now. Would they be able to find him in the dark? It must be close to bedtime. Warm inside his jacket and hood, he knew that if he lay down on the ground he wouldn't be so warm.

Then he remembered an experiment his dad had shown him. It was called *cold, cold ground*. There **was** a way to keep warm on the ground. They'd practiced it at school, with dolls.

He looked around for a good place to build a bed, and decided that the best place would be right against the log where he sat. He would be sheltered there. Now, could he find enough stuff quickly to make a bed? He remembered the teacher saying that it was important to set up a warm waiting place as quickly as possible, using whatever was close. If there was no suitable material nearby, he would be better off spending the time before dark looking for cover.

In a forest, though, there's usually enough stuff to make a bed.

Calvin began to gather branches with plenty of leaves and needles on them, and to arrange them against the log to form a mattress.

He also collected smaller bits of brush and dead sticks and leaves, which he put on top of the branches. He saved some branches to cover himself like a blanket, putting these in another pile beside the mattress.

Soon the mattress was thick enough for him to lie on without his body touching the cold ground. It was nearly dark now, and it seemed as though they weren't going to find him for a long time yet. He shouted, "Mom! Dad!" but there was no reply. He lay down on his mattress and covered himself with branches the way he'd learned. First his feet, then his legs, then his stomach and body, and last of all his head.

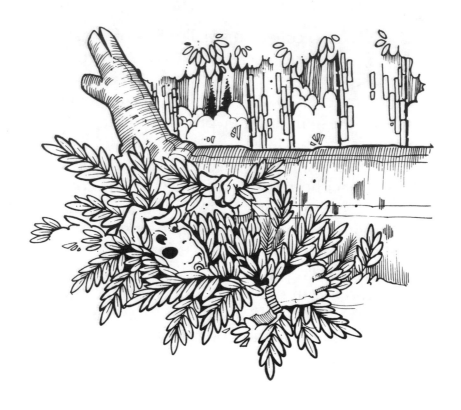

Now he would stay warm all night. Even if it rained, he would be fairly dry.

Lying there in the dark woods all alone, he remembered doing another experiment. *Buddy, buddy,* it was called. You curled up together with someone and it kept you warmer. He wished he had a friend with him now. The bed would help keep him warm, but another person or a pet would be much warmer and friendlier. Somewhere in the forest an owl called.

"Who . . . . Who . . . . Whoooooo!"
Calvin fell asleep.

The grown-ups hadn't forgotten Calvin, of course. His dad had searched near the campground in the dark until he began to think he might get lost, too. His mother had driven to the Ranger Station. Now the Search and Rescue people and the police were all ready to start looking for Calvin just as soon as it was light enough. They even had a helicopter there.

Calvin woke up.

It was daylight. The birds were singing. It took him a moment to realize where he was, then he pushed his branches aside and stood up. He was dry, and not really cold. The bed had worked just fine, but now he was hungry and thirsty.

He started off down a trail, thinking he might be able to find the campsite now it was lighter. He was thinking of bacon and eggs, not what they taught him at school.

Then he heard the rescue helicopter.

It passed right over the clearing but the men in it couldn't see Calvin, because he hadn't stayed put.

He was in the bushes a little way off, waving and shouting. They couldn't see him because of the trees. Next time, he would remember.

If you're lost you should stay in one place, if possible an open space, so that people who are looking for you can find you!

Calvin ran back to the middle of the clearing. He heard the helicopter coming again, but it had already searched this piece of forest without finding him. So it turned away, following a search pattern, looking somewhere else. Calvin was going to cry, but then decided it might be better to eat. He picked some berries from a nearby bush and looked at them. They were probably all right to eat, he thought. Or were they? He'd been making a lot of mistakes lately. Now he tried to remember what the teacher had said about eating and drinking.

Don't eat strange berries. It's better to be hungry for a while than to be sick.

Calvin threw the berries away. They might be poisonous, and in any case they didn't look very ripe. He didn't want to get a stomach-ache out here in the forest, with nobody to look after him. He was getting thirsty too, but he remembered the teacher saying, "Stay away from streams. Lost people often end up in trouble by falling in, when they're trying to get a drink. If you get really thirsty, lick water from the leaves."

So Calvin tried to forget his thirst, and stood there for a moment, wondering what else he could do.

Put out something bright so searchers can see where you are.

He didn't have a handkerchief but his T-shirt was white.

He started to take his jacket off.

This wasn't really a good idea even on a summer morning. He was better off keeping as warm as he could, so it was lucky that just at that moment he heard a shout.

"Haloooooooo!"

They were not far away!

He shouted back, "Here I am! Here I am! Here! Here!" He began to run in the direction of the shout, then suddenly he remembered. He'd better stay right where he was. So he stood there shouting, and soon there was a rustling in the bushes and a snapping of twigs, and a man stood there looking at him, smiling.

"Here he is!" the man shouted to his friends. "We've found him!" He knelt before Calvin. "You all right son?"

Calvin looked fine, so the volunteer searcher picked him up and started out toward the camp. Along the way they met the people from Search and Rescue who gave Calvin a drink of hot soup and covered him with a blanket. As they walked, the other searchers joined them, until by the time they reached the campground there was a whole crowd of them laughing and slapping each other on the back, and telling Calvin how clever he was to have looked after himself so well.

Then his mom and dad ran toward him
and hugged him and kissed him, much too
happy to be cross with him.

Behind them the forest stood tall and quiet and deep. Little trails ran through it, and animals used them. They knew where the trails led, and where the good food was, and the safe water. The animals knew all about the forest because it was their home. But it wasn't Calvin's home, and Calvin had to remember his lessons to be able to survive in there. If he hadn't remembered . . . who knows what might have happened?

"Whooooooooo?" asked the wise old owl.

Why Calvin Survived

Calvin survived because he remembered the lessons he'd been taught. Of course he didn't remember them **all** — who does? But he remembered enough to keep himself warm and safe, so that when the searchers came near he was still in good shape and able to shout and call attention to himself.

He remembered the lessons because of the way he'd been taught. He always enjoyed lessons where the teacher showed him things instead of just talking. His teacher had shown the class some experiments to prove why the rules made sense, and had planned activities to help the children learn how to help themselves. The teacher had brought people to the class too — people who knew about the outdoors, and knew how easy it was to get into danger if you didn't know what you were doing. The teacher had also asked parents to come along sometimes, and Calvin's parents had been to some of the talks.

But Calvin liked the experiments and the activities best. This is how the teacher did them.

Lid's On, Lid's Off

One day the teacher said, "I've noticed a lot of you haven't been wearing hats outside. It's been freezing out there. You all ought to be wearing something on your heads."

Jane said, "Hats are a nuisance."

"I've lost mine," said Wayne.

"All the same," said the teacher, "you should wear them. You never know when you might be standing in the cold longer than you expected. Maybe somebody forgot to pick you up. Maybe you got lost."

"I never get lost," said Calvin. "And anyway, my head never gets cold."

"It might not feel cold," said the teacher, "but you lose an awful lot of heat through your head. I'll prove it to you. Now, watch this."

She put two onion soup bowls on Calvin's desk.

Then she filled each one with hot water.

"Now," she said, "I'm going to put the lid on one bowl but not the other, see? Then we'll leave them for a while, say about fifteen minutes. And then we'll check to see which water is the warmer."

"I don't see how there can be any difference," said Calvin. "Water is water."

"Wait and see," said the teacher.

Fifteen minutes later she uncovered the bowl with the lid. Now the two bowls looked the same. "Take it in turn to feel the water," she said. "Tell me which is the warmer."

One by one, the children dipped their fingers in. "This one," said Jane. "This one," said Wayne.

"This is warmer," Calvin admitted. "The one that had the lid."

"So now you'll remember," said the teacher. "If you want to stay warm, don't forget to put on the lid. Wear you hat."
Calvin remembered.

Stop!

Before you read any further, try this activity with the children. Do not let them do it unsupervised.

You will need:
- 2 onion soup bowls with lids,
- 1 container filled with hot water.

Now you:
- Put equal amounts of very hot tap water in both bowls,
- Put the lid on one bowl and the lid beside the other bowl,
- Check in fifteen minutes time,
- Remove the lid. Compare the temperatures by feeling the water. By this time it's safe enough to touch.

Now discuss:
- Why one bowl stayed warmer,
- What people wear that is like a lid,
- What wearing a hat can do,
- What the children have to say about it.

Want to do some more?
Give each child a piece of paper and the following directions: Fold the paper in half. On one side draw the bowl with the lid, and on the other side draw the bowl without the lid. Ask the child which was the warmer. Write down the answers and discuss them with the child.

Cold, Cold Ground

"What did you learn at school today, Calvin?" his dad asked him. Calvin told him about the soup bowls and the lids.

"That's a good idea," said Calvin's mom, "teaching the children to look after themselves."

Calvin's dad had been thinking. "I have another idea," he said. He looked out of the window. It was dark outside, and quite cold. "There's something else you need to know when we go camping this summer. I'll show you why you shouldn't lie on the ground for very long."

"Who would want to?" Calvin asked. "Only animals."

"Well, you might get lost in the woods and have to stay out all night," his mother replied. "You'd feel tired and want to lie down, I'm sure. And if you lay on the bare ground for very long, you'd get terribly cold."

"I don't think I would," said Calvin. "You bought me a warm red jacket."

"Even so," said his dad, "you'd be surprised just how cold the ground can get at night, even in the summer."

He took a cookie tray from the kitchen and went outside. When he came back he'd filled the tray with earth. "Feel it, Calvin," he said.

Calvin did. "Brrr," he said. "It's cold."

"Now watch. I've got a styrofoam sheet here, about half as big as the tray." He put it on the tray so it covered half of the earth. Then he fetched two saucepans from the kitchen. He put one on the cold earth, and the other on top of the styrofoam so it didn't touch the earth. Then he filled both pans with hot water.

"Now we'll watch television for a while," he said.

About twenty minutes later, he said, "It's time we checked our experiment. Dip your fingers into each pan, Calvin, and tell me what you feel."

Calvin dipped his fingers in and said, "This one is colder."

"That's right," said his dad. "The one sitting on the earth is colder because the cold from the earth strikes up into the water. The one on the styrofoam pad is warmer because the pad insulates it from the earth and keeps the cold away. So even though we bought you a nice warm jacket, Calvin, it's better if you have something else between you and the ground. Cold strikes through clothes very quickly, remember."

"I'll remember," said Calvin.

"I'm sure you will," said his mom. "You can see how helpful it would be to find something to sit on, if you were lost. Can you think of anything that might be handy to sit on?"

"A styrofoam sheet," said Calvin.

His dad laughed. "You'd be lucky to find a styrofoam sheet in the forest. What else could you use?"

"If you could find some branches you could use them like a mattress."

"That's right, Calvin," said his dad. "And if there weren't any branches you could sit on a log. Anything to insulate you from the cold ground."

"Calvin has good ideas," said his mom. "If he ever did get lost, I know he'd use his head. He'd be all right."

"Dad has good ideas too," said Calvin. "Can he come to school and show his experiment to the rest of the kids?"

"I'd be glad to," said his dad.

Stop!

If you do this with the children now, it will help them remember!

You will need:
- 1 cookie tray filled with damp earth and kept in a freezer overnight,
- 2 containers for water,
- Very hot water,
- A sheet of styrofoam, approximately 1 cm. thick, and large enough to cover half the cookie tray.

Now you:
- Remove the cookie tray from the freezer,
- Let the children feel the earth,
- Place the styrofoam on half the cookie tray,
- Fill the containers with water,
- Place one container directly on the earth,
- Place the other container on the styrofoam sheet which is already on the earth,
- Check after twenty minutes,
- Feel the water in each container.

Now discuss:
- Which container of water stayed warmer, and why,
- What the experiment reminds you of in the story,
- What children could find out of doors for use as insulation,
- What the children have to say about it.

Want to do some more?
Provide drawing, painting and collage materials and ask each child to make a picture of the experiment. Make yourself available to write down comments made about the experiment, for subsequent discussion.

Build a Survival Bed for a Doll

"**N**ow, children," said the teacher, "we've learned why things stay warmer when they're covered, and we've learned that the ground is too cold to lie on for long. Next we must put these lessons together. First, I want you to think of a time when you might need to know these things."

"If I came home late at night and got locked out," said Nikki.

"I'm sure your mom and dad would let you in, Nikki. But all the same, the lessons might help. Anybody else?"

Calvin put up his hand. "If I got lost in the woods. Not that I ever would."

"Good, Calvin. Now, I want you to watch this." She went to the cupboard and took out a number of small branches, a watering can full of water, and two small dolls.

"Dolls?" said Calvin in disgust. "You want us to play with dolls?"

"I want you to pretend they're people," said the teacher. She put them on the table. "They're children who have wandered away from their parents on a camping trip, and got lost. One of them has learned from his lessons and the other hasn't. I want you to watch what happens to them."

"Is it dark?" asked Mandy, shivering. "Are there cougars?"

"It's dark, but there aren't any cougars. They've kept away because the children made a lot of noise. It's cold too, and now the children are tired, and they've got separated from each other. They want to lie down but the ground is too cold. So what do they do?"

"Those branches!" said Kevin.

"That's right. But only one of them remembered his lessons, right? Let's call him Calvin. Now, this is what Calvin did."

She made a little mattress out of the branches and placed the doll on it. Then she covered the doll with more branches.

"See, we've made a warm bed for Calvin. Now, watch this." She took the watering can and sprinkled water over the doll. "This is the rain. I'll rain on the other doll, too . . . There. Now," she took the Calvin-doll from its bed of branches and showed it to the class. "What do you notice about that?"

"Calvin is much drier," said Shannon.

"That's right. But the child who forgot his lessons is wet and cold, and very miserable."

The real Calvin looked at the two dolls. The teacher was right. The wet doll's hair was straggly and it **did** look miserable. He decided that if **he** ever got lost in the woods, it was worth remembering what he'd been taught.

Stop!

Do this activity together, right now!

You will need:
- 2 dolls,
- 15-20 small branches,
- 1 watering can or spray bottle,
- water.

Now you:
- Place the first doll on the floor or ground,
- Use 5 or 6 branches to make a ground cover and place the second doll on the branches. Place the rest of the branches with their tips towards the feet to make a cover for the doll,
- Sprinkle both dolls with equal amounts of water from the watering can.

Now discuss:
- Why one doll was dry,
- What else a person could do to stay warm and dry,
- What the children have to say about it.

Want to do some more?
- Leave the dolls in an area where the children can practice.
- Mark out an area in your yard, put out some branches and let the children play Survival.

Buddy, Buddy

"It's a nice day today," said the teacher, "so we'll go outside for a while." She opened the door and the class went out to the school yard. "Are you cold, Calvin?" she asked.

"Not really." The air was a bit cold but Calvin had his warm jacket on. It helped to keep the wind out.

"That's good. Now, I want each of you to choose partners."

The children did this — but in the end Calvin and Mandy were left together. "I don't want to be Mandy's partner," Calvin said. "Can't I be somebody else's?"

"And I don't want to be **your** partner, Calvin," said Mandy. "You put worms down people's backs."

"You won't have to be together, not for a while yet," said the teacher. "I want you all to go to separate places in the yard and wait there until I call you. Don't go near the edge of the yard."

Calvin walked away, glad that he didn't have to go with Mandy. She was bossy. He found himself a place to wait, near the middle of the yard where it was a bit damp and some rushes showed through the grass. It was not the kind of place Mandy would have liked. He found a flat rock and sat on it.

The other children were scattered all over the yard, sitting down. The wind was blowing quite hard where Calvin was, and he wondered if he would have been more comfortable behind the big tree nearby. He was getting lonely, too. It was queer how lonely it was, with all the other children so far away. It was quite cold too, in spite of his jacket.

Suddenly he heard the teacher calling out people's names, and telling them to sit with their partners. In a moment, Mandy came and sat beside him. "Sit close to your partners!" called the teacher.

And the funny thing was, he was glad to have Mandy there. Suddenly it was warmer and cosier. Mandy smiled at him. She said, "It's nicer like this."

After a while the teacher told them all to go and sit with their partners in the shelter of the hedge; and that was better still. The bushes kept the wind off them, and Mandy kept him company. Cuddled up to each other, they were both warmer. The teacher told them afterwards that this was another experiment which would help them find ways to keep warm, if they got lost.

Calvin remembered this, but most of all he remembered that Mandy was nice after all. They decided to be friends afterwards.

Stop!

Do it yourselves.

You will need no materials. You just go with a partner to an open space and try these activities:
- Sit close together,
- Sit far apart,
- Sit out in the field,
- Sit in a cozy spot.

Now discuss:
- What felt warmer,
- What felt better,
- When it would be helpful to remember this,
- What the children have to say about it.

Want to do some more?
Ask the children to paint or draw a forest scene and use this as a backdrop for puppets. Let the children create their own plays.

Find a Spot

"Today we're going to practise what we've learned," said the teacher. "We've done four experiments which show you how to keep warm and safe if you're lost. Now I want you to show me how much you remember. First, I want each of you to find a good survival spot in the classroom. You have two minutes. That's about as long as two T.V. commercials."

"But that's easy," said Terry. "Anywhere in the classroom is safe."

"Just pretend it's the forest," said the teacher. "Close your eyes for a moment and imagine the furniture is bushes and trees. Imagine the wind is blowing from the window towards the door. Imagine it's evening, and it's getting cold, and you're lost."

"Lynda will start crying soon," said Lisa.

"No, I won't," said Lynda. "And even if I did, it would only be pretending, to make it all more real."

So the children found their various survival spots around the classroom. Calvin sat under a desk which he pretended was a bush, and Shannon stood in a cupboard which she pretended was a hollow tree.

Ryan stood in the open, right in the middle of the classroom.

"Why did you choose that place?" asked Terry.

"I'm pretending there's a big spreading tree right over me," Ryan replied. He held out his hand. "Here's the trunk."

"Then you're standing on the wrong side of it, Ryan," said the teacher, "because I'm pretending the wind is blowing from the window towards the door, remember? You're standing in the wind."

Ryan moved to the other side of the invisible trunk. Then the teacher called the children to come and sit in a group. They talked about the spots they had picked and pointed out some good waiting places.

Next the teacher took them all out into the school yard. They all walked around the treed area while she showed them how far they could go. "Now you know all about finding a good survival spot," she said. "Go and find one in the schoolyard. Remember, the fence is the boundary."

They ran off. Terry crawled under a bush and Ryan slipped into the end of a hollow log. Lisa found a dry ditch and Lynda found a place among the roots of a big old tree. One by one the children found places where they would be snug and safe if they ever got caught outside. Calvin sat in a hollow under a sandy bank, sheltered from the wind and weather, until the teacher called all the children together.

As he walked back, Calvin thought, "Now I'll really know what to do if ever I get lost in the woods."

Stop!

Try the activity now.

Do it this way:
- Give the children two minutes to find survival spots in the classroom. Let them stay in their spots for one minute, then come together in a group.
- Take the children to a small open area you have checked out for safety. Make sure the area has clear boundaries. Adults or older children should mark the corners of the area. Give the children two minutes to find survival spots. Let them stay in the spot for five minutes. Bring them back to a group on a previously agreed signal.

Now discuss:
- What spots were found,
- Why certain spots were good,
- Why certain spots didn't work well,
- How the children felt,
- What the children have to say about it.

Want to do some more?

Have the children collect toy figures of people and vehicles. Encourage them to set up a forest in a sand box using twigs and small branches, and play Rescue.

Parents — Prepare That Child!

You are the best example your child has. Your choice of suitable clothing, your respect for the environment and your thoughtful behaviour will be a model for your child to follow. By rehearsing safety procedures with your child, you reinforce concepts that you have previously discussed, and you can find where your child's knowledge is lacking.

Rehearsal held under differing weather conditions will help direct your child's attention to matters of specific importance to your locality. For instance, children who live in a cold climate should be taught what to do when it snows.

Many children fear the dark. Talking about this may help, but it is far more effective to go with your child to the same spots in daylight, and in darkness. Try to build up their confidence.

Here are some further steps you can take to equip your child for the outdoors, particularly when camping in unfamiliar surroundings.

Boundaries.

The first step is to set the boundaries for exploration. This means accompanying the children and agreeing on actual landmarks. An outing which begins with a walk around the area to show the children how far they may go is less likely to result in problems than a vague instruction such as 'Don't go too far.'

Footprinting.

A few minutes devoted to footprinting each person can be time well spent in the event of the child getting lost. Place a sheet of aluminum foil on soft ground and have the child do a 'stork stand' on it to make an imprint of the shoe being worn. Label the print and put it in a safe place such as above the visor of your car. Even if the lost child has changed shoes, the impression will help the searchers to identify at least the size of footprint to look for.

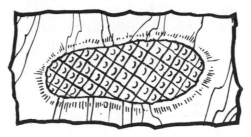

Clothing.

When buying a jacket, the choice of
• bright colours,
• a hood, and
• pockets
could help save the child's life. The bright colour will help make the child visible to searchers. The hood — even the small nylon hood in the collar of many jackets — will help keep in body heat essential to survival. Pockets provide a place to carry safety equipment and food. Even in hot summer weather, a jacket that folds into a small pouch can be belted around a child's waist without discomfort.

Emergency Pack.

Children who live in rural areas or who go camping should carry an emergency pack. A lightweight, inexpensive kit can be put together in a ziplock sandwich bag. It should contain:

A snack. This should be wrapped; recreation outlets have suitable concentrated food items. Remember that food attracts bears. It should therefore be completely sealed.

A whistle. Repeated shouting will weaken a child's voice so provide a whistle. It can be attached to a belt or clothing if not kept in the emergency pack. The child should be trained to call for help with three short blasts: Help! Help! Help! Whistles with a pea can become useless if the pea gets wet and swells. Dog training whistles are ideal.

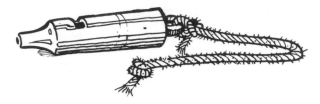

A reflector. A lid from a mason jar or a piece of foil provides a safe tool to attract attention visually. It will also keep the child occupied and therefore more likely to stay put. Do not use a glass mirror, which could cause a fire or cut the child.

Coloured strip. One or two strips of brightly coloured plastic (10 cm. by 100 cm.) will be useful for a lost child to tie to branches as markers, alerting searchers to the area where the child may be found. Orange garbage bags or kite plastic are suitable sources. Make the strips wide so they can't be confused with surveyor's tape.

Garbage bag. A garbage bag can serve as a tent for a child if it is slit before it is pulled over the head and body. (See Illustration) The slit serves as an opening for the face. Make sure you slit the bag before putting it in the emergency pack, and don't leave it around where a younger child might use it as a toy. Orange bags are more suitable than green because the colour contrasts with the surroundings.

Nevertheless, the best preparation for an emergency is the confidence your child will have gained by being encouraged to think independently and to solve problems within a safe and sympathetic environment.

Colleen's Letter

Dear Parents and Teachers,

Our story *Lost in the Woods* and the related activities are designed to help young children in a way which actively involves them in the learning process. Simply **telling** children what to do is not enough. It merely hands them a bunch of abstract ideas that float around in their heads like clouds. Using stories and activities helps children to take hold of these ideas and make them a part of their reality.

Hearing a story — and in the case of *Lost in the Woods*, seeing the film — causes children to become emotionally involved and provides a reason for them wanting to learn. Seeing a demonstration will reinforce what has been said, and inviting the child to participate will **personalize** the experience.

The same with talking. It is essential to talk **with** children, not **at** them. This means that the child should participate in the dialogue, expressing feelings and concerns. This helps the adult to learn which concepts the child understands, and which need further explanation.

To keep the conversation flowing it helps to ask 'open' rather than 'closed' questions. The question 'What did Calvin use to make his bed?' has only one answer — branches. If, on the other hand, you ask 'What kinds of things could you use to keep warm?' the children are invited to add their own thoughts — which can give a good indication of their degree of understanding.

As the children hear the story, participate in the activities, and take part in the discussions, they will become familiar with the ideas and **gain ownership** of them. It is this ownership that will lead a child to recreate the correct behaviour in a problem situation.

Earlier, I mentioned the film. This was made by the award-winning film-maker Barry Casson and it took three years to reach the screen, but when you see it I think you'll agree it's been worth the wait. It's the dramatic account of a young boy's survival after being lost overnight in the forest, is based on my own story and is of course titled *Lost in the Woods*. The 20 minute film was shot in the forests of British Columbia and was made with the co-operation of the National Film Board. For further information contact Barry Casson Film Productions, 895 Walfred Road, Victoria, B.C., Canada. V9C 2P1

And that's all for now. I hope you've enjoyed my book, and I hope the children in your care have enjoyed it too. Above all, I hope they learned from it, and will be able to enjoy our wilderness areas in safety as a result.

Take care,

Colleen